Meet the Designer

Nicoletta Tronci of NTmaglia Crochet Design finds serenity and inspiration working on Italy's beautiful Lake Como. She loves roomy tote bags and slouchy purses that combine traditional patterns and fanciful embroideries. "I was taught to crochet and knit by my grandmother when I was only 5 years old," she says. "I inherited from her the passion to translate imagination in handworks. ... I do not consider crochet as just a hobby or fancywork but more as an art to be enhanced in terms of creativity and professionalism." Her designs for stylish accessories appear internationally in popular crochet publications. Find out more on her website, ntmaglia-crochet.com, or on her NTmaglia page on Facebook, Etsy, Ravelry, and Craftsy.

Terrific Totes

Whether you are headed for the market or a matinee, you'll find a bag here that's just right!

M000267359

LEISURE ARTS, INC. • Maumelle, Arkansas

Caffè Latte Tote

INTERMEDIATE

Finished Measurements: 16½" wide x 13½" high (42 cm x 34.5 cm), excluding handles

SHOPPING LIST

Yarn (Medium Weight)
[1.8 ounces, 82 yards
(50 grams, 75 meters) per skein]:
- ☐ Off White - 7 skeins
- ☐ Brown - 5 skeins

Crochet Hook
- ☐ Size 7 (4.5 mm)
  or size needed for gauge

Additional Supplies
- ☐ Safety pins - 2
- ☐ 21" (53.5 cm) length cotton rope
  [½" (12 mm) diameter] - 2
- ☐ 14½" long x 1½" wide
  (37 cm x 4 cm) corrugated plastic
  strip to reinforce border - 2
- ☐ Yarn needle
- ☐ 1¹/₁₆" (27 mm) Button

GAUGE INFORMATION

16 sc and 18 rows/rnds = 4" (10 cm)

   In pattern, Rnds 7-11 = 2$\frac{1}{8}$" (5.5 cm)

Gauge Swatch: 4" (10 cm) square

With Off White, ch 17.

Row 1: Sc in second ch from hook and in each ch across: 16 sc.

Rows 2-18: Ch 1, turn; sc in each sc across.

Finish off.

——— STITCH GUIDE ———

TREBLE CROCHET

   (abbreviated tr)

YO twice, insert hook in st indicated, YO and pull up a loop (4 loops on hook), (YO and draw through 2 loops on hook) 3 times.

2-TR CLUSTER (uses next 3 sts)

YO twice, insert hook in next st, YO and pull up a loop (4 loops on hook), (YO and draw through 2 loops on hook) twice, YO twice, skip next st, insert hook in next st, YO and pull up a loop, (YO and draw through 2 loops on hook) twice, YO and draw through all 3 loops on hook.

3-TR CLUSTER (uses next 5 sts)

YO twice, insert hook in next st, YO and pull up a loop (4 loops on hook), (YO and draw through 2 loops on hook) twice, ★ YO twice, skip **next** st, insert hook in **next** st, YO and pull up a loop, (YO and draw through 2 loops on hook) twice; repeat from ★ once **more**, YO and draw through all 4 loops on hook.

CROSS ST (uses next 2 sts)

Skip next st, dc in next st, working **around** dc just made, dc in skipped st *(Fig. 5, page 46)*.

INSTRUCTIONS
Body

With Off White, ch 57.

Rnd 1 (Right side)**:** Sc in second ch from hook and in each ch across to last ch, 3 sc in last ch; working in free loops of beginning ch *(Fig. 2a, page 46)*, sc in next 54 chs, 2 sc in next ch; join with slip st to first sc: 114 sc.

Note: Loop a short piece of yarn around any stitch to mark Rnd 1 as **right** side.

Rnd 2: Ch 1, sc in same st as joining and in next 54 sc, 2 sc in each of next 3 sc, sc in next 54 sc, 2 sc in each of next 2 sc, sc in same st as first sc; join with sip st to first sc: 120 sc.

Rnd 3: Ch 1, sc in same st as joining and in next 54 sc, 2 sc in next sc, (sc in next sc, 2 sc in next sc) twice, sc in next 55 sc, 2 sc in next sc, (sc in next sc, 2 sc in next sc) twice; join with slip st to first sc: 126 sc.

Rnd 4: Ch 1, sc in same st as joining and in next 55 sc, 2 sc in next sc, (sc in next 2 sc, 2 sc in next sc) twice, sc in next 56 sc, 2 sc in next sc, (sc in next 2 sc, 2 sc in next sc) twice; join with slip st to first sc: 132 sc.

Rnd 5: Ch 1, sc in same st as joining and in each sc around; join with slip st to first sc.

Rnd 6: Ch 3 (**counts as first dc, now and throughout**), dc in next sc and in each sc around; join with slip st to first dc.

Rnd 7 (front)**:** Ch 4 (**counts as first tr, now and throughout**), skip next dc, work 2-tr Cluster, ch 5, skip next dc, ★ work 3-tr Cluster, ch 5, skip next dc; repeat from ★ around; skip first tr and join with slip st to next 2-tr Cluster: 22 Clusters and 22 ch-5 sps.

Rnd 8 (front): Ch 5 **(counts as first tr plus ch 1, now and throughout), turn**; skip next ch-5 sp, ★ (tr, ch 1) 3 times in next Cluster, skip next ch-5 sp; repeat from ★ around, (tr, ch 1) twice in same st as joining; join with slip st to first tr, place loop onto safety pin to keep piece from unraveling while working the next 2 rnds: 66 tr and 66 ch-1 sps.

Rnd 9 (background): With **wrong** side facing, working in **front** of previous 2 Off White rnds and in **each** dc 2 rnds **below** (on Rnd 6), join Brown with slip st in same st as joining (after beginning ch); ch 4, tr in next skipped dc, ★ skipping next Cluster leg, tr in same dc as Cluster leg and in next skipped dc; repeat from ★ around; join with slip st to first tr: 132 tr.

Rnd 10 (background): Ch 4, turn; working **behind** previous 2 Off White rnds, tr in next tr and in each tr around; join with slip st to first tr, place loop onto safety pin to keep piece from unraveling while working the next 2 rnds.

Rnd 11: With **wrong** side facing, slip Off White loop from safety pin onto hook, ch 3, turn; with **right** side facing, matching front tr and ch-1 sps with background tr and working through **both** layers, dc in next st and in each st around; join with slip st to first dc.

Rnd 12 (front): Ch 4, do **not** turn; skip next dc, work 2-tr Cluster, ch 5, skip next dc, ★ work 3-tr Cluster, ch 5, skip next dc; repeat from ★ around; skip first tr and join with slip st to next 2-tr Cluster: 22 Clusters and 22 ch-5 sps.

Rnd 13 (front): Ch 5, turn; skip next ch-5 sp, ★ (tr, ch 1) 3 times in next Cluster, skip next ch-5 sp; repeat from ★ around, (tr, ch 1) twice in same st as joining; join with slip st to first tr, place loop onto safety pin to keep piece from unraveling while working the next 2 rnds: 66 tr and 66 ch-1 sps.

Rnd 14 (background): With **wrong** side facing, slip Brown loop from safety pin onto hook, ch 4, working in **front** of previous 2 Off White rnds and in **each** dc 2 rnds **below**, tr in same st as joining (after beginning ch); tr in next skipped dc, ★ skipping next Cluster leg, tr in same dc as Cluster leg and in next skipped dc; repeat from ★ around; join with slip st to first tr: 132 tr.

Rnds 15-29: Repeat Rnds 10-14, 3 times: 132 tr.

Rnd 30 (background): Ch 4, turn; working **behind** previous 2 Off White rnds, tr in next tr and in each tr around; join with slip st to first tr, finish off.

Rnd 31: With **wrong** side facing, slip Off White loop from safety pin onto hook, ch 3, turn; with **right** side facing, matching front tr and ch-1 sps with background tr and working through **both** layers, dc in next st and in each st around; join with slip st to first dc, do **not** finish off.

Right side

Wrong side

BORDER

Rnd 1 (Wrong side)**:** Ch 1, turn; sc in each dc around; join with slip st to first sc: 132 sc.

Rnds 2-7: Ch 1, turn; skip first sc, sc in next sc and in each sc around; join with slip st to first sc: 126 sc.

Rnd 8 (turning ridge)**:** Ch 3, turn; working **around** first dc, dc in sc **before** joining st (**beginning Cross St made**), work Cross Sts around; join with slip st to first dc: 63 Cross Sts (126 dc).

Rnds 9-15: Ch 1, turn; sc in each st around; join with slip st to first sc.

Finish off, leaving a long end for sewing.

Button Loop

With Brown, ch 31; slip st in second ch from hook and in each ch across; finish off leaving a long end for sewing.

Matching free loops of beginning ch, fold Button Loop in half and sew free loops together, leaving a 1¼" (32 mm) opening. With Body of Tote lying flat, insert end of Button Loop between 2 Cross Sts on Border at center of one side of Tote and sew in place on wrong side.

Handle (Make 2)

With Brown, ch 83.

Row 1 (Wrong side)**:** Sc in second ch from hook and in each ch across: 82 sc.

Note: Mark the **back** of any stitch on Row 1 as **right** side.

Rows 2-6: Ch 1, turn; sc in each sc across.

Joining Row: With **right** side facing, slip st in end of each row across and in free loops of first 6 chs; place one length of cotton rope down the center of the **wrong** side of piece. Fold piece, matching free loops of beginning ch with tops of sc on Row 6. Working through **both** layers, slip st in next 70 sts; slip st in free loops of next 6 chs and in end of each row across; slip st in first sc on Row 6; finish off leaving a long end for sewing.

Repeat for second Handle.

Using photo as a guide for placement, sew first and last 6 sts at each end of Handle across Rnds 1-6 of Border, leaving center 5½" (14 cm) between ends (having joining row of each Handle toward the other).

Fold Border to **wrong** side along turning ridge (Rnd 8). Encasing corrugated plastic strips on each side of Body, sew sts on last round of Border in place to sts on Rnd 31 of Body.

Sew button to center front, opposite Button Loop.

Sunny Days Tote

Shown on page 9.

 **EASY**

Finished Measurements: 15½" wide x 12½" high (39.5 cm x 32 cm), excluding handles

SHOPPING LIST

Yarn (Medium Weight)
[1.8 ounces, 82 yards
(50 grams, 75 meters) per skein]:
- ☐ Grey - 4 skeins
- ☐ Lime - 2 skeins
- ☐ Off White - 2 skeins
- ☐ Rose - 2 skeins

Crochet Hook
- ☐ Size 7 (4.5 mm)

  or size needed for gauge

Additional Supplies
- ☐ 16" (40.5 cm) length cotton rope
  [½" (12 mm) diameter] - 2
- ☐ 14" long x 1½" wide (35.5 cm x 4 cm)
  corrugated plastic strip to reinforce
  border - 2
- ☐ Yarn needle

GAUGE INFORMATION

16 sc and 18 rows/rnds = 4" (10 cm)

Gauge Swatch: 4" (10 cm) square

With Grey, ch 17.

Row 1: Sc in second ch from hook and in each ch across: 16 sc.

Rows 2-18: Ch 1, turn; sc in each sc across.

Finish off.

STITCH GUIDE

FRONT POST SINGLE CROCHET

(abbreviated FPsc)

Insert hook from **front** to **back** around post of sc indicated *(Fig. 4, page 46)*, YO and pull up a loop, YO and draw through both loops on hook.

CROSS ST (uses next 2 sts)

Skip next st, dc in next st, working **around** dc just made, dc in skipped st *(Fig. 5, page 46)*.

INSTRUCTIONS
Body

With Grey, ch 50.

Rnd 1 (Right side)**:** Sc in second ch from hook and in each ch across to last ch, 4 sc in last ch; working in free loops of beginning ch *(Fig. 2a, page 46)*, sc in next 47 chs, 3 sc in next ch; join with slip st to first sc: 102 sc.

Note: Loop a short piece of yarn around any stitch to mark Rnd 1 as **right** side.

Rnd 2: Ch 1, turn; sc in first 2 sc, 2 sc in next sc, sc in next 47 sc, 2 sc in next sc, sc in next 2 sc, 2 sc in next sc, sc in next 47 sc, 2 sc in last sc; join with slip st to first sc: 106 sc.

Rnd 3: Ch 1, turn; 2 sc in first sc, sc in next 49 sc, 2 sc in next sc, sc in next 2 sc, 2 sc in next sc, sc in next 49 sc, 2 sc in next sc, sc in last 2 sc; join with slip st to first sc: 110 sc.

Rnd 4: Ch 1, turn; sc in first 3 sc, 2 sc in next sc, sc in next 49 sc, 2 sc in next sc, sc in next 4 sc, 2 sc in next sc, sc in next 49 sc, 2 sc in next sc, sc in last sc; join with slip st to first sc: 114 sc.

Rnd 5: Ch 1, turn; sc in first sc, 2 sc in next sc, sc in next 51 sc, 2 sc in next sc, sc in next 4 sc, 2 sc in next sc, sc in next 51 sc, 2 sc in next sc, sc in last 3 sc; join with slip st to first sc: 118 sc.

Rnd 6: Ch 1, turn; work FPsc around each sc around; join with slip st to first FPsc.

Rnds 7-10: Ch 1, turn; sc in each st around; join with slip st to first sc, at end of last rnd, finish off.

Rnd 11: With **right** side facing, 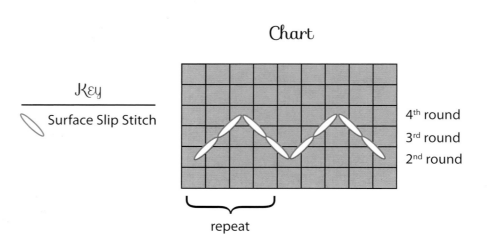 join Lime with sc in same st as joining *(see Joining With Sc, page 45)*; sc in each sc around; join with slip st to first sc.

Rnds 12-15: Repeat Rnds 7-10.

Rnd 16: With **wrong** side facing, join Off White with sc in same st as joining; sc in next 5 sc, 2 sc in next sc, sc in next 58 sc, 2 sc in next sc, sc in last 52 sc; join with slip st to first sc: 120 sc.

Rnds 17-20: Repeat Rnds 7-10.

Rnd 21: With **right** side facing, join Rose with sc in same st as joining; sc in each sc around; join with slip st to first sc.

Rnds 22-26: Ch 1, turn; sc in each sc around; join with slip st to first sc, at end of last rnd, finish off.

Rnds 27-32: With Lime, repeat Rnds 21-26.

Rnd 33: With Off White, repeat Rnd 21.

Rnds 34-36: Ch 1, turn; sc in each sc around; join with slip st to first sc.

Rnd 37: Ch 1, turn; sc in first 55 sc, 2 sc in next sc, sc in next 59 sc, 2 sc in next sc, sc in last 4 sc; join with slip st to first sc: 122 sc.

Rnd 38: Ch 1, turn; sc in each sc around; join with slip st to first sc, finish off.

Rnds 39-51: Repeat Rnds 21-33.

Rnd 52: Ch 1, turn; sc in first 7 sc, 2 sc in next sc, sc in next 60 sc, 2 sc in next sc, sc in last 53 sc; join with slip st to first sc: 124 sc.

Rnds 53-56: Repeat Rnds 7-10.

BORDER
Rnd 1: With **right** side facing, join Grey with sc in same st as joining; sc in each sc around; join with slip st to first sc.

Rnds 2-6: Ch 1, turn; sc in each sc around; join with slip st to first sc.

Rnd 7 (turning ridge)**:** Ch 3 (**counts as first dc**), turn; working **around** first dc, dc in sc **before** joining st (**beginning Cross St made**), work Cross Sts around; join with slip st to first dc: 62 Cross Sts (124 dc).

Rnds 8-13: Ch 1, turn; sc in each st around; join with slip st to first sc.

Finish off, leaving a long end for sewing.

With Grey, following chart and beginning at side of tote, 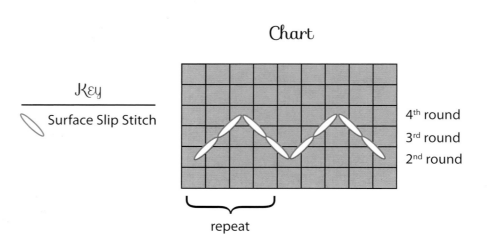 work surface slip sts *(Figs. 7a-c, page 47)* on the 2nd, 3rd & 4th Off White rounds of each Off White stripe.

Chart

Key

⟍ Surface Slip Stitch

4th round
3rd round
2nd round

repeat

Handle (Make 2)

With Grey, ch 70.

Row 1 (Right side): Sc in second ch from hook and in each ch across: 69 sc.

Note: Mark Row 1 as **right** side.

Rows 2-7: Ch 1, turn; sc in each sc across.

Finish off, leaving a long end for sewing.

Place one length of cotton rope down the center of the **wrong** side of piece. Fold piece, matching tops of sc on Row 7 with free loops of beginning ch. Working through **both** layers, skip first 7 sts and join Grey with slip st in next st; slip st in each st across to last 7 sts, leave remaining 7 sts unworked; finish off.

Repeat for second Handle.

Using photo as a guide for placement, sew first and last 6 sts at each end of Handle across top Off White stripe, leaving center 5" (12.5 cm) between ends (having joining row of each Handle toward the other).

Fold Border to **wrong** side along turning ridge (Rnd 7). Encasing corrugated plastic strips on each side of Body, sew sts on last round of Border in place to sts on Rnd 1.

Terra Cotta Tote

EASY +

Finished Measurements: 16" wide x 13" high (40.5 cm x 33 cm), excluding handles

SHOPPING LIST

Yarn (Medium Weight)

[1.8 ounces, 82 yards
(50 grams, 75 meters) per skein]:

- ☐ Beige - 10 skeins
- ☐ Brown - 2 skeins

Crochet Hook

- ☐ Size 7 (4.5 mm)

  or size needed for gauge

Additional Supplies

- ☐ 20" (51 cm) length cotton rope
  [½" (12 mm) diameter] - 2
- ☐ 16" long x 1½" wide (40.5 cm x 4 cm)
  corrugated plastic strip to reinforce
  border - 2
- ☐ Yarn needle
- ☐ 1¼" (32 mm) Button

GAUGE INFORMATION

One Square = 3¼" (8.25 cm)

16 sc and 18 rows = 4" (10 cm)

Gauge Swatch: 3¼" (8.25 cm) square

Work same as Square: 44 sc.

── STITCH GUIDE ──

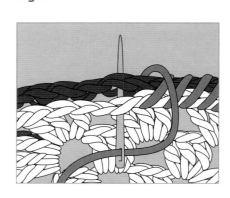 **CROSS ST** (uses next 2 sts)

Skip next st, dc in next st, working **around** dc just made, dc in skipped st *(Fig. 5, page 46).*

INSTRUCTIONS

Body (Make 2)

SQUARE (Make 15)

With Beige, ch 5; join with slip st to form a ring.

Rnd 1 (Right side)**:** Ch 1, 16 sc in ring; join with slip st to first sc.

Note: Loop a short piece of yarn around any stitch to mark Rnd 1 as **right** side.

Rnd 2: Ch 4 (**counts as first dc plus ch 1**), (dc in next sc, ch 1) around; join with slip st to first dc: 16 dc and 16 ch-1 sps.

Rnd 3: Ch 1, 2 sc in each ch-1 sp around; join with slip st to first sc: 32 sc.

Rnd 4: Ch 3 (**counts as first dc, now and throughout**), hdc in next sc, sc in next 4 sc, hdc in next sc, dc in next sc, ★ ch 3, dc in next sc, hdc in next sc, sc in next 4 sc, hdc in next sc, dc in next sc; repeat from ★ 2 times **more**, ch 1, hdc in first dc to form last ch-3 sp: 32 sts and 4 ch-3 sps.

Rnd 5: Ch 1, 2 sc in last ch-3 sp made, sc in next 8 sts, (3 sc in next ch-3 sp, sc in next 8 sts) around, sc in same sp as first sc; join with slip st to first sc, finish off leaving a long end for sewing: 44 sc.

Assembly

Forming 3 horizontal strips of 5 Squares each, 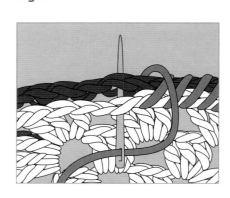 whipstitch Squares together as follows:

Thread yarn needle with long end from one Square. With **wrong** sides of 2 Squares together and beginning in center sc of corner, insert the needle from **front** to **back** through **both** loops on **both** pieces *(Fig. A).* Bring the needle around and insert it from **front** to **back** through the next loops on both pieces. Continue in this manner across, ending in center sc of next corner and keeping the sewing yarn fairly loose.

With Beige, whipstitch strips together in same manner.

Fig. A

TOP BORDER

Row 1: With **right** side of long edge facing,  join Beige with sc in center sc of first corner *(see Joining With Sc, page 45)*; sc in next 11 sc, (sc in same sc as joining on next square and in next 11 sc) 4 times: 60 sc.

Row 2: Ch 3, turn; work Cross Sts across to last sc, dc in last sc: 29 Cross Sts and 2 dc.

Rows 3-10: Ch 1, turn; sc in each st across: 60 sc.

Front Only - Row 11 (turning ridge)**:** Ch 3, turn; work Cross Sts across to last sc, dc in last sc: 29 Cross Sts and 2 dc.

Back Only - Row 11 (turning ridge)**:** Ch 3, turn; work 14 Cross Sts, ch 2, skip next 2 sc (Button Loop opening), work 14 Cross Sts, dc in last sc: 28 Cross Sts, 2 dc, and 2 chs.

Rows 12-18: Ch 1, turn; sc in each st across: 60 sc.

Finish off, leaving a long end for sewing.

BOTTOM BAND

Row 1: With **right** side of opposite long edge facing, join Beige with sc in center sc of first corner; sc in next 11 sc, (sc in same st as joining on next square and in next 11 sc) 4 times: 60 sc.

Rows 2-8: Ch 1, turn; sc in each sc across.

Finish off, leaving a long end for sewing.

With **wrong** sides of Body pieces together, matching sts on Row 8 of Bottom Band and using long end, whipstitch bottom seam.

Side Band

With Beige, ch 40.

Row 1 (Wrong side)**:** Sc in back ridge *(Fig. 1, page 45)* of second ch from hook and each ch across: 39 sc.

Note: Mark the back of any stitch on Row 1 as **right** side.

Rows 2-15: Ch 1, turn; sc in each sc across.

Joining Row: Ch 1, turn; with **wrong** sides of Row 15 and joined strips of first Body together, and working through **both** loops on **both** pieces, slip st in each st across; having **wrong** sides of row ends on Side Band and Bottom Bands together, and working through **both** pieces, slip st evenly across; with **wrong** sides of free loops of beginning ch *(Fig. 2b, page 46)* and joined strips of second Body together, and working through **both** loops on **both** pieces, slip st in each st across; finish off.

TRIM

With **right** side of Side Band facing, join Beige with slip st in end of Row 15, ch 1; working from **left** to **right**, work reverse sc *(Figs. 6a-d, page 46)* evenly across end of rows; finish off.

Repeat on opposite side of Body across Second Side Band.

Button Loop

With Brown and leaving a long end for sewing, ch 31.

Row 1 (Right side)**:** Sc in back ridge of second ch from hook and each ch across: 30 sc.

Row 2: Ch 1, do **not** turn; working from **left** to **right**, work reverse sc in each sc across; finish off leaving a long end for sewing.

Matching free loops of beginning ch, fold Button Loop in half and sew free loops together, leaving a 1³/₈" (35 mm) opening. With **right** side facing, insert base of joined area through Button Loop opening on Row 11 of Top Border and sew in place on **wrong** side.

Handle (Make 2)

With Brown and leaving a long end for sewing, ch 81.

Row 1 (Right side)**:** Sc in back ridge of second ch from hook and each ch across: 80 sc.

Note: Mark Row 1 as **right** side.

Rows 2-6: Ch 1, turn; sc in each sc across.

Finish off, leaving a long end for sewing.

Place one length of cotton rope down the center of the **wrong** side of piece. Fold piece, matching tops of sc on Row 6 with free loops of beginning ch. Working through **both** layers, skip first 7 sts and join Brown with slip st in next st; slip st in each st across to last 7 sts, leave remaining 7 sts unworked; finish off.

Repeat for second Handle.

Using photo as a guide for placement, sew first and last 6 sts at each end of Handle across Rows 4-9 of Top Border, leaving center 5" (12.5 cm) between ends (having joining row of each Handle toward the other).

Fold Top Borders to **wrong** side along turning ridge (Row 11). Encasing corrugated plastic strips, sew sts on last row of Border in place to sts on Row 3; then sew end of rows together on each side.

Sew button to center front, opposite Button Loop.

Twill Weave Tote

Shown on page 19.

 **INTERMEDIATE**

Finished Measurements: 18" wide x 13" high (45.5 cm x 33 cm), excluding handles

SHOPPING LIST

Yarn (Medium Weight)

[1.8 ounces, 82 yards
(50 grams, 75 meters) per skein]:

☐ Gold - 12 skeins

☐ Brown - 1 skein

Crochet Hook

☐ Size 7 (4.5 mm)

or size needed for gauge

Additional Supplies

☐ 24" (61 cm) length cotton rope
[½" (12 mm) diameter] - 2

☐ 17" long x 1½" wide
(43 cm x 4 cm) corrugated plastic
strip to reinforce border - 2

☐ Yarn needle

GAUGE INFORMATION

16 sc and 18 rows/rnds = 4" (10 cm)

In pattern, 18 sts and 6 rows = 4½" (11.5 cm)

Gauge Swatch: 4" (10 cm) square

With Gold, ch 17.

Row 1: Sc in second ch from hook and in each ch across: 16 sc.

Rows 2-18: Ch 1, turn; sc in each sc across.

Finish off.

STITCH GUIDE

TREBLE CROCHET *(abbreviated tr)*

YO twice, insert hook in st indicated, YO and pull up a loop (4 loops on hook), (YO and draw through 2 loops on hook) 3 times.

FRONT POST TRIPLE TREBLE CROCHET

(abbreviated FPtr tr)

YO 4 times, insert hook from **front** to **back** around post of st indicated *(Fig. 4, page 46)*, YO and pull up a loop (6 loops on hook), (YO and draw through 2 loops on hook) 5 times.

BACK POST TRIPLE TREBLE CROCHET

(abbreviated BPtr tr)

YO 4 times, insert hook from **back** to **front** around post of st indicated *(Fig. 4, page 46)*, YO and pull up a loop (6 loops on hook), (YO and draw through 2 loops on hook) 5 times.

CROSS ST (uses next 2 sts)

Skip next st, dc in next st, working **around** dc just made, dc in skipped st *(Fig. 5, page 46)*.

INSTRUCTIONS

First Side

BOTTOM

With Gold, ch 61.

Row 1 (Right side)**:** Sc in second ch from hook and in each ch across: 60 sc.

Note: Loop a short piece of yarn around any stitch to mark Row 1 as **right** side.

Rows 2-6: Ch 1, turn; sc in each sc across.

BODY

Row 1: Ch 4 (**does not count as a st**), turn; skip first 3 sc, work FPtr tr around each of next 3 sc, working in **front** of last 3 FPtr tr made, work FPtr tr around each of 3 skipped sc, skip next 3 sc, work FPtr tr around each of next 3 sc, ★ working in **front** of last 3 FPtr tr made, work FPtr tr around each of 3 skipped sc, skip next 3 sc, work FPtr tr around each of next 3 sc; repeat from ★ across, working in **front** of last 3 FPtr tr made, work FPtr tr around each of first 2 skipped sc, YO 4 times, insert hook from **front** to **back** around post of 3rd skipped sc, YO and pull up a loop (6 loops on hook), (YO and draw through 2 loops on hook) 4 times (2 loops on hook), YO twice, insert hook in last sc of previous row (already worked into), YO and pull up a loop (5 loops on hook), (YO and draw through 2 loops on hook) twice, YO and draw through all 3 loops on hook.

Row 2: Ch 4 (**counts as first st**), turn; skip first st, tr in next 2 sts, ★  skip next 3 sts, work BPtr tr around each of next 3 sts, working **behind** last 3 BPtr tr made, work BPtr tr around each of 3 skipped sts; repeat from ★ across to last 3 sts, tr in last 3 sts.

Row 3: Ch 4 (**does not count as a st**), turn; skip first 3 sts, work FPtr tr around each of next 3 sts, ★ working in **front** of last 3 FPtr tr made, work FPtr tr around each of 3 skipped sts, skip next 3 sts, work FPtr tr around each of next 3 sts; repeat from ★ across, working in **front** of last 3 FPtr tr made, work FPtr tr around each of first 2 skipped sts, YO 4 times, insert hook from **front** to **back** around post of 3rd skipped st, YO and pull up a loop (6 loops on hook), (YO and draw through 2 loops on hook) 4 times (2 loops on hook), YO twice, insert hook in last tr of previous row (already worked into), YO and pull up a loop (5 loops on hook), (YO and draw through 2 loops on hook) twice, YO and draw through all 3 loops on hook.

Rows 4-14: Repeat Rows 2 and 3, 5 times; then repeat Row 2 once **more**.

Finish off.

Second Side

BOTTOM

Row 1: With **wrong** side of First Side Bottom facing and working in free loops of beginning ch *(Fig. 2a, page 46)*, join Gold with sc in first ch *(see Joining With Sc, page 45)*; sc in each ch across: 60 sc.

Rows 2-5: Ch 1, turn; sc in each sc across.

BODY

Work same as First Side.

Side Band

Row 1: With **right** side of Bottom facing, join Gold with sc in end of first row; work 8 sc evenly spaced across end of rows: 9 sc.

Rows 2-12: Ch 1, turn; sc in each sc across.

Row 13 (Increase row)**:** Ch 1, turn; sc in first sc, 2 sc in next sc, sc in each sc across to last 2 sc, 2 sc in next sc, sc in last sc: 11 sc.

Rows 14-37: Repeat Rows 2-13 twice: 15 sc.

Rows 38-48: Ch 1, turn; sc in each sc across; at end of Row 48, finish off.

Repeat on opposite end of Bottom.

With Gold, sew Side Bands to each Body.

Border

Rnd 1: With **right** side facing, join Gold with sc in first sc of Side Band; ★ sc in each sc across Band, sc in each st across Body; repeat from ★ once **more**; join with slip st to first sc: 150 sc.

Rnd 2: Ch 3 (**counts as first dc, now and throughout**), turn; working **around** first dc, dc in sc **before** joining st (**beginning Cross St made**), work Cross Sts around; join with slip st to first dc: 75 Cross Sts (150 dc).

Rnd 3: Ch 1, do **not** turn; sc in each dc around; join with slip st to first sc.

Rnds 4-8: Ch 1, turn; sc in each sc around; join with slip st to first sc.

Rnd 9 (turning ridge)**:** Ch 3, turn; working **around** first dc, dc in sc **before** joining st (**beginning Cross St made**), work Cross Sts around; join with slip st to first dc: 75 Cross Sts (150 dc).

Rnds 10-15: Ch 1, turn; sc in each st around; join with slip st to first sc.

Finish off, leaving a long end for sewing.

Handle (Make 2)

With Brown, ch 81.

Row 1 (Right side)**:** Sc in second ch from hook and in each ch across: 80 sc.

Note: Mark Row 1 as **right** side.

Rows 2-7: Ch 1, turn; sc in each sc across.

Place one length of cotton rope down the center of the **wrong** side of piece. Fold piece matching tops of sc on Row 7 with free loops of beginning ch. Working through **both** layers, skip first 7 sts and join Brown with slip st in next st; slip st in each st across to last 7 sts, leave remaining 7 sts unworked; finish off.

Repeat for second Handle.

Using photo as a guide for placement, sew first and last 6 sts at each end of Handle across Rnds 3-8 of Border, leaving center 5½" (14 cm) between ends (having joining row of each Handle toward the other).

Fold Border to **wrong** side along turning ridge (Rnd 9). Encasing corrugated plastic strips on each side of Body, sew sts on last row of Border in place to sts on Rnd 2.

Sublime Stripes Shoulder Bag

 **INTERMEDIATE +**

Finished Measurements: 14½" wide x 12" high (37 cm x 30.5 cm), excluding handle

SHOPPING LIST

Yarn (Medium Weight)

[1.8 ounces, 82 yards
(50 grams, 75 meters) per skein]:

☐ Brown - 4 skeins
☐ Orange (CC1) - 1 skein
☐ Rose (CC2) - 1 skein
☐ Lavender (CC3) - 1 skein
☐ Lime (CC4) - 1 skein
☐ Aqua (CC5) - 1 skein

Crochet Hook

☐ Size 7 (4.5 mm)
   or size needed for gauge

Additional Supplies

☐ Safety pins - 2
☐ Yarn needle
☐ 1¼" (32 mm) Button

GAUGE INFORMATION

In Body pattern,

16 sts and 7 rnds = 4" (10 cm)

In Flap pattern, (sc, ch 1) 10 times

(20 sts) and 20 rows = 4" (10 cm)

📹 **Gauge Swatch:** 3¾" wide x 4" tall

(9.5 cm x 10 cm) flattened

With Brown, ch 16; place marker in fourth ch from hook for st placement. Work same as Body through Rnd 7: 16 dc and 16 ch-1 sps. Finish off.

Right side

Wrong side

INSTRUCTIONS
Body

The Body is worked in one piece. Each round is worked in 2 steps, creating a double layer of fabric, with the **wrong** side of the Body facing throughout.

With Brown, ch 60; place marker in fourth ch from hook for st placement.

Rnd 1 - Step 1 (front)**:** Dc in sixth ch from hook **(5 skipped chs count as first dc plus ch 1 and one skipped ch)**, ch 1, skip next ch, † dc in next ch, ch 1, skip next ch †; repeat from † to † across to last ch, (dc, ch 1) 3 times in last ch; working in 📹 free loops of beginning ch *(Fig. 2a, page 46)*, skip next ch, repeat from † to † across to marked ch, (dc, ch 1) twice in marked ch, remove marker; join with slip st to first dc, place loop onto safety pin to keep piece from unraveling while working the next step, drop Brown to the front (toward you): 60 dc and 60 ch-1 sps.

Rnd 1 - Step 2 (back)**:** With **front** facing, working **behind** Brown sts in Step 1 **and** in skipped chs on beginning ch, 📹 join Orange with dc in first skipped ch *(see Joining With Dc, page 45)*; ch 1, † (dc in next skipped ch, ch 1) across to end 3-dc group, (skip **next** dc, dc in same ch as 3-dc group, ch 1) twice †;

working in free loops of skipped chs across opposite side of beginning ch, repeat from † to † once; move Brown to the back (away from you), then with Orange, join with slip st to first dc, place loop onto safety pin to keep piece from unraveling while working the next step, drop Orange to the back (away from you).

Rnd 2 - Step 1: With **front** facing, slip Brown loop from safety pin onto hook; picking up Brown strand **before** Orange strand, ch 4 **(counts as first dc plus ch 1)**, Brown will "wrap" last ch made on previous step, working in Brown dc **and** through corresponding ch-1 sp of previous step (through both layers), dc in next dc keeping loop with safety pin and Orange strand **before** dc, ch 1, (dc in next dc, ch 1) around; join with slip st to first dc, place loop onto safety pin to keep piece from unraveling while working the next step, drop Brown to the front.

Rnd 2 - Step 2: With **front** facing and working **behind** Brown sts in Step 1, slip Orange loop from safety pin onto hook; ch 4, (dc in next Orange dc, ch 1) around; move Brown to the back, then join with slip st to first dc, place loop onto safety pin to keep piece from unraveling while working the next step, drop Orange to the back.

Rnds 3 and 4: Repeat Rnd 2 twice; at end of Step 2 on Rnd 4, finish off Orange ONLY.

For the next 16 rounds, Step 1 will ALWAYS be worked with Brown and Step 2 will be worked with a CC in the following stripe sequence: 4 rnds **each** Rose, Lavender, Lime and Aqua.

Rnd 5 - Step 1: With **front** facing, slip Brown loop from safety pin onto hook; picking up Brown strand **before** CC strand, ch 4, Brown will "wrap" last ch made on previous step, working in Brown dc **and** through corresponding ch-1 sp of previous step (through both layers), dc in next dc keeping loop with safety pin and CC strand **before** dc, ch 1, (dc in next dc, ch 1) around; join with slip st to first dc, place loop onto safety pin to keep piece from unraveling while working the next step, drop Brown to the front.

Rnd 5 - Step 2: With **front** facing and working **behind** Brown sts in Step 1, join next CC with dc in same CC dc as joining on previously worked Step 2; ch 1, (dc in next CC dc, ch 1) around; move Brown to the back, then join with slip st to first dc, place loop onto safety pin to keep piece from unraveling while working the next step, drop CC to the back.

Rnd 6 - Step 1: With **front** facing, slip Brown loop from safety pin onto hook; picking up Brown strand **before** CC strand, ch 4, Brown will "wrap" last ch made on previous step, working in Brown dc **and** through corresponding ch-1 sp of previous step (through both layers), dc in next dc keeping loop with safety pin and CC strand **before** dc, ch 1, (dc in next dc, ch 1) around; join with slip st to first dc, place loop onto safety pin to keep piece from unraveling while working the next step, drop Brown to the front.

Rnd 6 - Step 2: With **front** facing and working **behind** Brown sts in Step 1, slip CC loop from safety pin onto hook; ch 4, (dc in next CC dc, ch 1) around; move Brown to the back, then join with slip st to first dc, place loop onto safety pin to keep piece from unraveling while working the next step, drop CC to the back.

Rnds 7 and 8: Repeat Rnd 6 twice; at end of Step 2 on last rnd, finish off CC ONLY.

Rnds 9-20: Continuing in stripe sequence on Step 2, repeat Rnds 5-8, 3 times; do **not** finish off Brown.

BORDER

Rnd 1 - Step 1: With **front** facing, slip Brown loop from safety pin onto hook; picking up Brown strand **before** CC strand, ch 4, Brown will "wrap" last ch made on previous step, working in Brown dc **and** through corresponding ch-1 sp of previous step (through both layers), dc in next dc keeping loop with safety pin and CC strand **before** dc, ch 1, (dc in next dc, ch 1) around; join with slip st to first dc, place loop onto safety pin to keep piece from unraveling while working the next step, drop Brown to the front.

Rnd 1 - Step 2: With **front** facing and working **behind** Brown sts in Step 1, join second Brown with dc in same Aqua dc as joining on previously worked Step 2; ch 1, (dc in next Aqua dc, ch 1) around; move first Brown to the back, then join with slip st to first dc, place loop onto safety pin to keep piece from unraveling while working the next step, drop second Brown to the back.

Rnd 2 - Step 1: With **front** facing, slip first Brown loop from safety pin onto hook; picking up first Brown strand **before** second Brown strand, ch 4, Brown will "wrap" last ch made on previous step, working in first Brown dc **and** through corresponding ch-1 sp of previous step (through both layers), dc in next dc keeping second Brown loop and strand **before** dc, (ch 1, dc in next dc) around to last 2 dc, place a marker in last dc made for Flap placement, ch 1, (dc in next dc, ch 1) twice; join with slip st to first dc, finish off first Brown.

Rnd 2 - Step 2: With **front** facing and working **behind** first Brown sts in Step 1, slip second Brown loop from safety pin onto hook; ch 4, (dc in next second Brown dc, ch 1) around; join with slip st to first dc, finish off.

Turn Body **right** side out.

FLAP

Row 1: With **right** side facing and working through **both** layers (in ch-1 sps **and** dc), 📹 join Brown with sc in marked dc *(see Joining With Sc, page 45)*, remove marker; ★ ch 1, skip next st, sc in next st; repeat from ★ 26 times **more**, place a marker around next st for Strap placement and leave remaining sts unworked: 28 sc and 27 ch-1 sps.

Row 2: Ch 1, turn; sc in first sc and in next ch-1 sp, ch 1, (sc in next ch-1 sp, ch 1) across to last ch-1 sp, sc in last ch-1 sp and in last sc: 29 sc and 26 ch-1 sps.

Row 3: Ch 1, turn; sc in first sc, ch 1, (sc in next ch-1 sp, ch 1) across to last 2 sc, skip next sc, sc in last sc: 28 sc and 27 ch-1 sps.

Rows 4-10: Repeat Rows 2 and 3, 3 times; then repeat Row 2 once **more**: 29 sc and 26 ch-1 sps.

Row 11 (Decrease row)**:** Ch 1, turn; sc in first sc, skip next sc, sc in next ch-1 sp, (ch 1, sc in next ch-1 sp) across to last 2 sc, skip next sc, sc in last sc: 28 sc and 25 ch-1 sps.

Row 12: Ch 1, turn; sc in first sc, ch 1, (sc in next ch-1 sp, ch 1) across to last 2 sc, skip next sc, sc in last sc: 27 sc and 26 ch-1 sps.

Rows 13 and 14: Repeat Rows 2 and 3: 27 sc and 26 ch-1 sps.

Row 15 (Decrease row)**:** Ch 1, turn; skip first sc, sc in next ch-1 sp, (ch 1, sc in next ch-1 sp) across to last sc, leave last sc unworked: 26 sc and 25 ch-1 sps.

Row 16: Ch 1, turn; sc in first sc and in next ch-1 sp, ch 1, (sc in next ch-1 sp, ch 1) across to last ch-1 sp, sc in last ch-1 sp and in last sc: 27 sc and 24 ch-1 sps.

Rows 17 and 18: Repeat Rows 11 and 12: 25 sc and 24 ch-1 sps.

Rows 19 and 20: Repeat Rows 15 and 16: 25 sc and 22 ch-1 sps.

Rows 21 and 22: Repeat Rows 11 and 12: 23 sc and 22 ch-1 sps.

Rows 23-25: Ch 1, turn; skip first sc, sc in next ch-1 sp, (ch 1, sc in next ch-1 sp) across to last sc, leave last sc unworked: 20 sc and 19 ch-1 sps.

Row 26 (Decrease row)**:** Turn; slip st in next ch-1 sp, ch 1, sc in next sc and in next ch-1 sp, ch 1, (sc in next ch-1 sp, ch 1) across to last 2 ch-1 sps, sc in next ch-1 sp and in next sc, leave remaining sts unworked: 19 sc and 16 ch-1 sps.

Row 27 (Decrease row)**:** Turn; skip first sc, slip st in next sc, (ch 1, sc in next ch-1 sp) across to last 2 sc, leave last 2 sc unworked: 16 sc and 15 ch-1 sps.

Rows 28 and 29: Repeat Rows 26 and 27: 12 sc and 11 ch-1 sps.

Row 30: Turn; slip st in next ch-1 sp and in next sc, (ch 1, sc in next ch-1 sp) across to last ch-1 sp, leave remaining sts unworked; finish off: 9 sc and 8 ch-1 sps.

EDGING

Row 1: With **right** side facing, join Brown with slip st in same st on Body as first sc on Row 1 of Flap, ch 1; sc evenly along entire edge of Flap to keep piece lying flat; slip st in same st on Body as last sc on Row 1 of Flap.

Row 2: Ch 1, do **not** turn; working from **left** to **right**, work reverse sc in each sc across *(Figs. 6a-d, page 46)*; slip st in same st as joining on Row 1.

Row 3: Working in sts on Row 1 of Edging, work Surface slip st in each st across *(Fig. 7a, page 47)*; finish off.

BUTTON LOOP

With Brown, ch 17; sc in second ch from hook and in each ch across; finish off leaving a long end for sewing: 16 sc.

Thread yarn needle with end and, being careful not to twist Button Loop, fold Loop having tops of sc matching. Sew first and last 3 sc together.

Centering Button Loop on wrong side of Flap, sew to top of sts on Row 29. Sew Button to Body corresponding to Button Loop.

Strap

The Strap is a braid made up of 6 chains. 2 Chains are joined to each of 3 sts on the Body, beginning in the marked st as follows:

With **right** side facing, join Brown with slip st in st; make a chain approximately 70" (178 cm) long; finish off.

Divide the chains into 3 double-chain sections and braid until you have a length of approximately 37" (94 cm), or to desired length. Secure the braid and sew to the opposite side of Body.

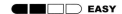

Arabesque Clutch

◖■□▷ **EASY**

Finished Measurements: 10½" wide x 6" high (26.5 cm x 15 cm)

SHOPPING LIST

Yarn (Medium Weight)

[1.8 ounces, 82 yards
(50 grams, 75 meters) per skein]:

☐ Black - 6 skeins

☐ Off White - 1 skein

Crochet Hook

☐ Size 7 (4.5 mm)

or size needed for gauge

Additional Supplies

☐ 11" (28 cm) Zipper

☐ Yarn needle

☐ Sewing needle and
matching thread

GAUGE INFORMATION

16 sc and 18 rows = 4" (10 cm)

Gauge Swatch: 4" (10 cm) square

With Black, ch 17.

Row 1: Sc in second ch from hook and in each ch across: 16 sc.

Rows 2-18: Ch 1, turn; sc in each sc across.

Finish off.

——— STITCH GUIDE ———

FRONT POST SINGLE CROCHET
(abbreviated FPsc)

Insert hook from **front** to **back** around post of stitch indicated *(Fig. 4, page 46)*, YO and pull up a loop, YO and draw through both loops on hook.

SINGLE CROCHET 2 TOGETHER
(abbreviated sc2tog)

Pull up a loop in each of next 2 sc, YO and draw through all 3 loops on hook **(counts as one sc).**

INSTRUCTIONS
Bottom

With Black, ch 43.

Row 1 (Right side)**:** Sc in back ridge of second ch from hook *(Fig. 1, page 45)* and each ch across: 42 sc.

Note: Loop a short piece of yarn around any stitch to mark Row 1 as **right** side.

Rows 2-9: Ch 1, turn; sc in each sc across.

Front

Row 1 (Turning ridge)**:** Ch 1, turn; work FPsc around each sc across.

Rows 2-24: Ch 1, turn; sc in each st across.

TOP

Row 1 (Turning ridge)**:** Ch 1, turn; work FPsc around each sc across.

Rows 2 and 3: Ch 1, turn; sc in each st across.

Finish off.

Back

Row 1: With **wrong** side of opposite side of Bottom facing and working around sc on Row 1, join Black with FPsc around first sc *(see Joining With FPsc, page 45)*; work FPsc around each st across: 42 FPsc.

Rows 2-24: Ch 1, turn; sc in each st across.

Place a marker in top of last sc made for Flap placement.

TOP

Row 1 (Turning ridge)**:** Ch 1, turn; work FPsc around each sc across.

Rows 2 and 3: Ch 1, turn; sc in each st across.

Finish off.

Flap

Foundation Row: With **right** side facing and Top of Back toward you, join Black with sc in marked sc *(see Joining With Sc, page 45)*; sc in each sc across Row 24 of Back: 42 sc.

Row 1 (Right side)**:** Turn; slip st in first 3 sc, ch 1, sc in next 36 sc, leave remaining 3 sc unworked.

Rows 2-20: Ch 1, turn; sc in each sc across.

Row 21: Ch 1, turn; sc in first sc, sc2tog, sc in each sc across to last 3 sc, sc2tog, sc in last sc: 34 sc.

Row 22: Ch 1, turn; sc in each sc across.

Rows 23-26: Ch 1, turn; sc in first sc, sc2tog, sc in each sc across to last 3 sc, sc2tog, sc in last sc: 26 sc.

Row 27: Turn; slip st in first 3 sc, ch 1, sc in next 20 sc, leave remaining 3 sc unworked; finish off: 20 sc.

EDGING

Row 1: With **right** side facing and leaving a long end for sewing, join Black with sc in end of Row 1; sc evenly along entire edge of Flap to keep piece lying flat.

Rows 2 and 3: Ch 1, turn; sc in each sc across; at end of Row 3, finish off leaving a long end for sewing.

Using long ends, sew ends of Edging to first and last 3 sts on Foundation Row.

With **right** side facing, using Off White and working in sc on Row 1 of Edging, work Surface slip st in each sc across *(Figs. 7a-c, page 47)*. Repeat, working in sc on Row 2 of Edging.

With **right** side facing, using Off White and working in sc indicated on Chart, work Surface slip st on Flap, beginning in second sc on Row 1.

Side Band

Row 1: With **right** side of Bottom facing, join Black with sc in end of first row; work 10 sc evenly spaced across end of rows: 11 sc.

Rows 2-8: Ch 1, turn; sc in each sc across.

Row 9 (Decrease row)**:** Ch 1, turn; sc in first sc, sc2tog, sc in each sc across to last 3 sc, sc2tog, sc in last sc: 9 sc.

Rows 10-17: Repeat Rows 2-9: 7 sc.

Rows 18-24: Ch 1, turn; sc in each sc across; at end of Row 24, finish off.

Repeat on opposite end of Bottom.

Assembly

With Black, sew Side Bands to Front and Back; then sew end of rows on Tops to Side Bands.

TOP OPENING

With **right** side facing, join Black with slip st in any st on Row 3 of either Top, ch 1; working from **left** to **right** in sts around entire opening, 🎥 work reverse sc *(Figs. 6a-d, page 46)* in each st around; join with slip st to first st, finish off.

Using sewing needle and matching thread, sew zipper into the Top opening.

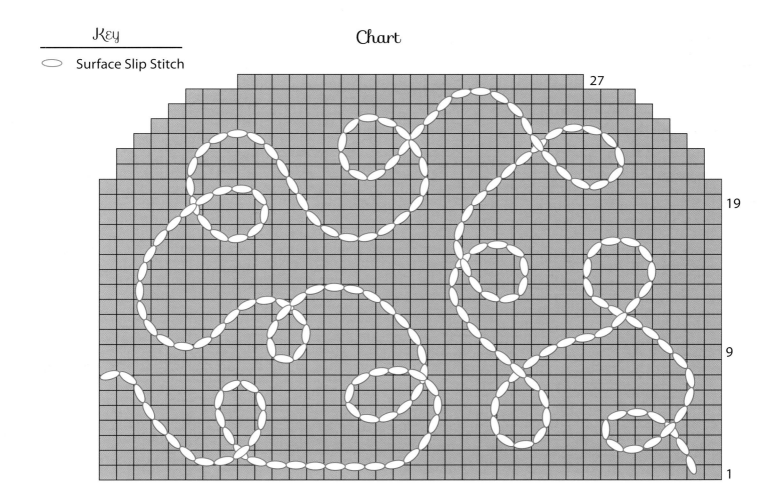

Key

⬭ Surface Slip Stitch

Chart

27

19

9

1

All-Day Shoulder Bag

 **INTERMEDIATE**

Finished Measurements: 13" wide x 12" high (33 cm x 30.5 cm), excluding strap

SHOPPING LIST

Yarn (Medium Weight)
[1.8 ounces, 82 yards
(50 grams, 75 meters) per skein]:
- ☐ Blue - 8 skeins
- ☐ Brown - 2 skeins

Crochet Hook
- ☐ Size 7 (4.5 mm)

  or size needed for gauge

Additional Supplies
- ☐ 12½" (32 cm) Zipper
- ☐ Yarn needle
- ☐ Sewing needle and
  matching thread

GAUGE INFORMATION

16 sc and 18 rows/rnds = 4" (10 cm)

Gauge Swatch:

3¾" (9.5 cm) diameter

Work same as Square thru Rnd 4: 48 sts (8 triangles).

─── STITCH GUIDE ───

🎬 TREBLE CROCHET

(abbreviated tr)

YO twice, insert hook in st or sp indicated, YO and pull up a loop (4 loops on hook), (YO and draw through 2 loops on hook) 3 times.

🎬 DOUBLE TREBLE CROCHET

(abbreviated dtr) (uses one st)

YO 3 times, insert hook in st indicated, YO and pull up a loop (5 loops on hook), (YO and draw through 2 loops on hook) 4 times.

🎬 BEGINNING CLUSTER

(uses first st)

Ch 3, ★ YO, insert hook in st indicated, YO and pull up a loop, YO and draw through 2 loops on hook; repeat from ★ once **more**, YO and draw through all 3 loops on hook.

🎬 CLUSTER (uses one st)

★ YO, insert hook in st indicated, YO and pull up a loop, YO and draw through 2 loops on hook; repeat from ★ 2 times **more**, YO and draw through all 4 loops on hook.

🎬 SINGLE CROCHET 2 TOGETHER

(abbreviated sc2tog)

Pull up a loop in each of next 2 sc, YO and draw through all 3 loops on hook **(counts as one sc)**.

🎬 DOUBLE TREBLE CROCHET 5 TOGETHER

(abbreviated dtr5tog)

★ YO 3 times, insert hook in **next** dtr, YO and pull up a loop, (YO and draw through 2 loops on hook) 3 times; repeat from ★ 4 times **more**, YO and draw through all 6 loops on hook **(counts as one dtr)**.

🎬 CROSS ST (uses next 2 sts)

Skip next st, dc in next st, working **around** dc just made, dc in skipped st *(Fig. 5, page 46)*.

─────────

INSTRUCTIONS

Panel (Make 2)

SQUARE

With Blue, ch 5; join with slip st to form a ring.

Rnd 1 (Right side)**:** Ch 3 **(counts as first dc, now and throughout)**, 15 dc in ring; join with slip st to first dc: 16 dc.

Note: Loop a short piece of yarn around any stitch to mark Rnd 1 as **right** side.

Rnd 2: Ch 1, 2 sc in same st as joining and in each dc around; join with slip st to first sc: 32 sc.

Rnd 3: Work Beginning Cluster in same st as joining, ch 2, skip next sc, ★ work Cluster in next sc, ch 2, skip next sc; repeat from ★ around; join with slip st to top of Beginning Cluster: 16 Clusters and 16 ch-2 sps.

Rnd 4: Ch 6, sc in second ch from hook, hdc in next ch, dc in next ch, tr in next ch, dtr in next ch, skip next Cluster, ★ slip st in next Cluster, ch 6, sc in second ch from hook, hdc in next ch, dc in next ch, tr in next ch, dtr in next ch, skip next Cluster; repeat from ★ around; join with slip st to first slip st: 48 sts (8 triangles).

Rnd 5: Ch 5 **(counts as first dtr)**, 4 dtr in same st as joining, ch 2, slip st in ch at tip of next triangle, ch 2, skip next 5 sts, ★ 5 dtr in next slip st (between triangles), ch 2, slip st in ch at tip of next triangle, ch 2, skip next 5 sts; repeat from ★ around; join with slip st to first dtr: 40 dtr, 8 slip sts, and 16 ch-2 sps.

Rnd 6: Ch 1, sc in same st as joining and in next 4 dtr, ★ † 2 dc in next ch-2 sp, dc in next slip st, 2 tr in next ch-2 sp, ch 4, dtr5tog, ch 4, 2 tr in next ch-2 sp, dc in next slip st, 2 dc in next ch-2 sp †, sc in next 5 dtr; repeat from ★ 2 times **more**, then repeat from † to † once; join with slip st to first sc: 64 sts and 8 ch-4 sps.

Rnd 7: (Slip st, work Beginning Cluster) in next sc, ch 1, (skip next st, work Cluster in next st, ch 1) 4 times, tr in next ch-4 sp, (3 tr, ch 3, 3 tr) in next dtr, tr in next ch-4 sp, ch 1, ★ work Cluster in next tr, ch 1, (skip next st, work Cluster in next st, ch 1) 7 times, tr in next ch-4 sp, (3 tr, ch 3, 3 tr) in next dtr, tr in next ch-4 sp, ch 1; repeat from ★ 2 times **more**, (work Cluster in next st, ch 1, skip next st) 3 times; join with slip st to top of Beginning Cluster: 100 sts (25 per side) and 4 corner ch-3 sps.

Rnd 8: Slip st in next ch, ch 3, working **around** first dc, dc in same st as joining st (**beginning Cross St made**), work 6 Cross Sts, (3 dc, ch 3, 3 dc) in next corner ch-3 sp, skip next dc, ★ work 12 Cross Sts, (3 dc, ch 3, 3 dc) in next corner ch-3 sp, skip next dc; repeat from ★ 2 times **more**, work 5 Cross Sts; join with slip st to first dc: 120 dc (30 dc per side) and 4 corner ch-3 sps.

Rnd 9: Slip st in next dc, ch 3, working **around** first dc, dc in same st as joining st (**beginning Cross St made**), work 7 Cross Sts, skip next dc, (3 dc, ch 3, 3 dc) in next corner ch-3 sp, skip next dc, ★ work 14 Cross Sts, skip next dc, (3 dc, ch 3, 3 dc) in next corner ch-3 sp, skip next dc; repeat from ★ 2 times **more**, work 6 Cross Sts; join with slip st to first dc, finish off: 136 dc (34 dc per side) and 4 corner ch-3 sps.

FIRST EDGE

Row 1: With **right** side facing, 🎥 join Blue with dc in center ch of next corner ch-3 sp *(see Joining With Dc, page 45)*; ★ skip next dc, work Cluster in next dc, ch 1; repeat from ★ across to next corner ch-3 sp, dc in center ch of corner ch-3: 36 sts.

Row 2: Ch 3, turn; work Cross Sts across to last dc, dc in last dc: 36 dc.

Row 3: Ch 3, turn; work Cluster in next dc, ★ ch 1, skip next dc, work Cluster in next dc; repeat from ★ across to last 2 dc, skip next dc, dc in last dc; finish off: 35 sts.

SECOND EDGE

Work same as First Edge on opposite side of Square; do **not** finish off.

TOP BORDER

Row 1: Ch 1, do **not** turn; with **right** side facing, work 2 sc in end of each row on Second Edge, sc in next sp, sc in next 34 dc, sc in next sp, work 2 sc in end of each row on First Edge: 48 sc.

Rows 2 and 3: Ch 1, turn; sc in each sc across.

First Side - Row 1 (Wrong side)**:** Ch 1, turn; sc in first 12 sc, leave remaining 36 sc unworked.

Row 2: Turn; slip st in first 2 sc, sc in next sc and in each sc across: 10 sc.

Row 3: Ch 1, turn; sc in first 8 sc, leave remaining 2 sc unworked: 8 sc.

Row 4: Turn; slip st in first 2 sc, sc in next sc and in each sc across: 6 sc.

Row 5: Ch 1, turn; sc in first 4 sc, leave remaining 2 sc unworked: 4 sc.

Row 6: Turn; slip st in first sc, sc in last 3 sc; finish off.

Second Side - Row 1: With **wrong** side facing, skip next 24 sc and 🎥 join Blue with sc in next sc *(see Joining With Sc, page 45)*; sc in next 11 sc: 12 sc.

Row 2: Ch 1, turn; sc in first 10 sc, leave remaining 2 sc unworked: 10 sc.

Row 3: Turn; slip st in first 2 sc, sc in next sc and in each sc across: 8 sc.

Row 4: Ch 1, turn; sc in first 6 sc, leave remaining 2 sc unworked: 6 sc.

Row 5: Turn; slip st in first 2 sc, sc in next sc and in each sc across: 4 sc.

Row 6: Ch 1, turn; sc in first 3 sc, slip st in last sc; finish off.

BOTTOM

Row 1: With **right** side facing, join Blue with sc in end of Row 3 on First Edge; sc in same row, 2 sc in each of next 2 rows, sc in next sp, sc in next 34 dc, sc in next sp, work 2 sc in end of each row on Second Edge: 48 sc.

Rows 2-8: Ch 1, turn; sc in each sc across.

Finish off, leaving a long end for sewing on one Panel only.

Thread yarn needle with long end. With **right** sides together and matching sts on Row 8 of Bottom, whipstitch Bottom of Panels together working through inside loops *(Fig. A)*.

Fig. A

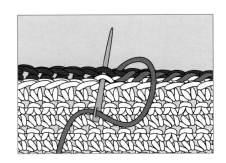

Side Band

Row 1: With **right** side of Bottom facing and working in end of rows (16 rows total), skip first 2 rows and join Blue with sc in next row; sc in next 11 rows: 12 sc.

Rows 2-14: Ch 1, turn; sc in each sc across.

Row 15 (Decrease row)**:** Ch 1, turn; sc in first sc, sc2tog, sc in each sc across to last 3 sc, sc2tog, sc in last sc: 10 sc.

Rows 16-43: Repeat Rows 2-15 twice: 6 sc.

Rows 44-52: Ch 1, turn; sc in each sc across; at end of Row 52, finish off.

Repeat on opposite end of Bottom.

With Blue, sew Side Bands to Panels, sewing through back loops of clusters and chains when sewing Panel to edge of Side Band.

Panel Trim

Row 1: With **right** side of one Panel facing, join Blue with sc in first sc on Row 6 of first side; work 10 sc evenly spaced across first side to unworked sc of Top Border, sc in each unworked sc across, work 11 sc evenly spaced across second side ending in last sc on Row 6: 46 sc.

Rows 2 and 3: Ch 1, turn; sc in each sc across.

Row 4: Ch 1, do **not** turn; working from **left** to **right**, work reverse sc in each sc across *(Figs. 6a-d, page 46)*; finish off.

Repeat Rows 1-4 on second Panel.

With Blue, sew end of rows of Panel Trim to last row of Side Bands.

Using sewing needle and matching thread, sew zipper into Panel Trim opening.

Strap

With Brown, ch 6.

Row 1 (Right side): Working in  back ridge of beginning ch *(Fig. 1, page 45)* sc in second ch from hook **(skipped ch counts as first sc)** and in each ch across: 6 sc.

Note: Mark Row 1 as **right** side.

Row 2: Ch 1 **(counts as first sc)**, turn; sc in next sc and in each sc across.

Repeat Row 2 until Strap measures approximately 40" (101.5 cm) from beginning ch, ending by working a **right** side row.

Finish off.

With **right** side facing, using Blue and working in second st from each edge when working vertically, and in top of sts on Row 1 and on second-to-last row when working horizontally, work Surface slip st around entire Strap *(Figs. 7a-c, page 47)*; cut yarn leaving a 6" (15 cm) end, finish off by pulling loop though last slip st. Thread yarn needle with end and insert needle under loop of first slip st, then back down through last slip st made; secure end on wrong side of work.

Using photo as a guide for placement, sew 3½" (9 cm) of each end of Strap to Side Bands.

Tassel

Cut a piece of cardboard 4" (10 cm) square. Wind Brown yarn around the cardboard approximately 20 times. Cut an 18" (45.5 cm) length of Brown yarn and insert it under all of the strands at the top of the cardboard; pull up **tightly** and tie securely, leaving the yarn ends long. Cut the yarn at the opposite end of the cardboard *(Fig. A)* and then remove it. Cut an 8" (20.5 cm) length of Brown yarn and wrap it **tightly** around the Tassel 3 or 4 times, approximately ¾" (19 mm) below the top *(Fig. B)*; tie securely. Trim the ends.
Attach Tassel to zipper pull with long ends.

Fig. A

Fig. B

Shabby Rose Tote

 **EASY +**

Finished Measurements: 17" wide x 14" high (43 cm x 35.5 cm), excluding handles

SHOPPING LIST

Yarn (Medium Weight)
[1.8 ounces, 82 yards
(50 grams, 75 meters) per skein]:
- ☐ 9 skeins

Crochet Hook
- ☐ Size 7 (4.5 mm)
  or size needed for gauge

Additional Supplies
- ☐ 24" (61 cm) length cotton rope
  [½" (12 mm) diameter] - 2
- ☐ 16½" long x 1½" wide (42 cm x 4 cm)
  corrugated plastic strip to reinforce
  border - 2
- ☐ Yarn needle

GAUGE INFORMATION

In pattern, 8 Cross Sts (16 sts)
and 8 rows = 4" (10 cm)
16 sc and 18 rows/rnds = 4" (10 cm)
Gauge Swatch: 4" wide x 4¼" high
(10 cm x 10.75 cm)
Ch 17.

Row 1: Sc in second ch from hook
and in each ch across: 16 sc.

Rows 2-9: Ch 3 (**counts as first dc**),
turn; work Cross Sts across to last st,
dc in last st.
Finish off.

STITCH GUIDE

TREBLE CROCHET
(abbreviated tr)

YO twice, insert hook in st indicated,
YO and pull up a loop (4 loops on
hook), (YO and draw through 2 loops
on hook) 3 times.

CROSS ST (uses next 2 sts)

Skip next st, dc in next st, working
around dc just made, dc in skipped st
(Fig. 5, page 46).

FRONT POST SINGLE CROCHET
(abbreviated FPsc)

Insert hook from **front** to **back** around
post of sc indicated *(Fig. 4, page 46)*,
YO and pull up a loop, YO and draw
through both loops on hook.

BACK POST SINGLE CROCHET
(abbreviated BPsc)

Insert hook from **back** to **front** around
post of sc indicated *(Fig. 4, page 46)*,
YO and pull up a loop, YO and draw
through both loops on hook.

INSTRUCTIONS
Body

Ch 54.

Rnd 1 (Right side)**:** Sc in second ch
from hook and in each ch across to
last ch, 3 sc in last ch; working in
 free loops of beginning ch *(Fig. 2a,
page 46)*, sc in next 51 chs, 2 sc in
next ch; join with slip st to first sc:
108 sc.

Note: Loop a short piece of yarn
around any stitch to mark Rnd 1 as
right side.

Rnd 2: Ch 1, turn; 2 sc in each of first
2 sc, sc in next 51 sc, 2 sc in each of
next 3 sc, sc in next 51 sc, 2 sc in last
sc; join with slip st to first sc: 114 sc.

Rnd 3: Ch 1, turn; 2 sc in first sc, sc
in next 52 sc, 2 sc in next sc, (sc in
next sc, 2 sc in next sc) twice, sc in
next 52 sc, (2 sc in next sc, sc in next
sc) twice; join with slip st to first sc:
120 sc.

Rnd 4: Ch 1, turn; sc in first sc, 2 sc in
next sc, sc in next 2 sc, 2 sc in next sc,
sc in next 53 sc, 2 sc in next sc, (sc in
next 2 sc, 2 sc in next sc) twice, sc in
next 53 sc, 2 sc in next sc, sc in last sc;
join with slip st to first sc: 126 sc.

Rnd 5: Ch 1, turn; sc in first 2 sc, 2 sc
in next sc, sc in next 54 sc, 2 sc in
next sc, (sc in next 3 sc, 2 sc in next
sc) twice, sc in next 54 sc, 2 sc in next
sc, sc in next 3 sc, 2 sc in next sc, sc
in last sc; join with slip st to first sc:
132 sc.

Rnd 6: Ch 1, turn; sc in first 4 sc, 2 sc in next sc, sc in next 60 sc, 2 sc in next sc, sc in next 4 sc, 2 sc in next sc, sc in next 60 sc, 2 sc in last sc; join with slip st to first sc: 136 sc.

Rnds 7 and 8: Ch 1, turn; sc in each sc around; join with slip st to first sc.

Rnd 9: Ch 3 (**counts as first dc, now and throughout**), turn; working **around** first dc, dc in sc **before** joining st (**beginning Cross St made**), work Cross Sts around; join with slip st to first dc: 68 Cross Sts (136 dc).

Rnds 10-24: Ch 3, turn; working **around** first dc, dc in sc **before** joining (**beginning Cross St made**), work Cross Sts around; join with slip st to first dc.

BORDER

Rnd 1: Ch 1, turn; sc in first dc, ch 1, skip next dc, ★ sc in next dc, ch 1, skip next dc; repeat from ★ around; join with slip st to first sc: 68 sc and 68 ch-1 sps.

Rnd 2: Ch 1, turn; sc in same st as joining, ch 1, (sc in next sc, ch 1) around; join with slip st to first sc.

Rnd 3 (trim)**:** Do **not** turn; (slip st in next ch-1 sp, 5 dc in next ch-1 sp) around; join with slip st to first slip st: 34 5-dc groups.

Rnd 4 (Right side)**:** Ch 1, **turn**; with trim toward you and working in ch-1 sps on Rnd 1, (slip st, ch 1, sc) in first ch-1 sp, ch 1, (sc in next ch-1 sp, ch 1) around; join with slip st to first sc: 68 sc and 68 ch-1 sps.

Rnd 5: Ch 1, turn; work FPsc around same st as joining, ch 1, (work FPsc around next sc, ch 1) around; join with slip st to first FPsc.

Rnds 6-19: Ch 1, turn; sc in first ch-1 sp, ch 1, (sc in next ch-1 sp, ch 1) around; join with slip st to first sc.

Rnd 20 (trim)**:** Do **not** turn; (slip st in next ch-1 sp, 5 dc in next ch-1 sp) around; join with slip st to first slip st: 34 5-dc groups.

Rnd 21 (Right side)**:** Ch 1, **turn**; with trim toward you and working in ch-1 sps on Rnd 18 (following each sc made on Rnd 19), (slip st, ch 1, sc) in first ch-1 sp, ch 1, (sc in next ch-1 sp, ch 1) around; join with slip st to first sc: 68 sc and 68 ch-1 sps.

Rnd 22: Ch 1, turn; work FPsc around same st as joining, ch 1, (work FPsc around next sc, ch 1) around; join with slip st to first FPsc.

Rnd 23: Ch 1, turn; 5 dc in next FPsc, (slip st in next FPsc, 5 dc in next FPsc) around; join with slip st to turning ch.

Rnd 24: Ch 1, do **not** turn; working around sc on Rnd 18, work BPsc around first sc, ch 1, (work BPsc around next sc, ch 1) around; join with slip st to first sc: 136 sts (68 sc and 68 chs).

Rnd 25: Ch 1, do **not** turn; sc in same st as joining and in next 3 sts, skip next st, (sc in next 5 sts, skip next st) twice, ★ sc in next 4 sts, skip next st, (sc in next 5 sts, skip next st) twice; repeat from ★ around; join with slip st to first sc: 112 sc.

Rnds 26 and 27: Ch 1, **turn**; sc in each sc around; join with slip st to first sc.

Rnd 28 (turning ridge)**:** Ch 3, turn; working **around** first dc, dc in sc **before** joining **(beginning Cross St made)**, ★ work 11 Cross Sts, ch 2, skip next 2 sc (first handle opening); repeat from ★ once **more**, work 15 Cross Sts, ch 2, skip next 2 sc (second handle opening), work 11 Cross Sts, ch 2, skip next 2 sc (second handle opening), work 3 Cross Sts; join with slip st to first dc: 52 Cross Sts (104 dc) and 4 ch-2 sps.

Rnd 29: Ch 1, turn; sc in each dc around working 2 sc in each ch-2 sp; join with slip st to first sc: 112 sc.

Rnds 30-32: Ch 1, turn; sc in each sc around; join with slip st to first sc.

Finish off, leaving a long end for sewing.

Handle (Make 2)

Leaving a long end for sewing, ch 81.

Row 1 (Wrong side)**:** Sc in second ch from hook and in each ch across: 80 sc.

Note: Mark the **back** of any stitch on Row 1 as **right** side.

Rows 2-7: Ch 1, turn; sc in each sc across.

Joining Row: Ch 1, turn; place one length of cotton rope down the center of the **wrong** side of piece. Fold piece, matching top of sc on Row 7 with free loops of beginning ch. Working through **both** layers, slip st in each st across; finish off leaving a long end for sewing.

With **right** side facing on one side of Body, insert approximately 3 sts of each end of Handle through opening (having joining row of each Handle toward the other) and sew ends in place on **wrong** side.

Repeat for second Handle.

Fold Border to **wrong** side along turning ridge (Rnd 28). Encasing corrugated plastic strips on each side of Body, sew sts on last round of Border in place to sts on Rnd 16.

Roses

LARGE ROSE (Make 4)

Ch 36.

Row 1: Dc in sixth ch from hook (**5 skipped chs count as first dc plus ch 2**), ★ skip next 2 chs, (dc, ch 2, dc) in next ch; repeat from ★ across: 11 ch-2 sps.

Row 2 (Right side)**:** Ch 3, turn; 4 dc in first ch-2 sp, skip next dc, slip st in ▒ sp **before** next dc *(Fig. 3, page 46)*, (5 dc in next ch-2 sp, skip next dc, slip st in sp **before** next dc) twice, 7 dc in next ch-2 sp, ★ skip next dc, slip st in sp **before** next dc, 7 dc in next ch-2 sp; repeat from ★ across, slip st in last dc; finish off if desired, **or** work one or two leaves as follows:
† Ch 9, slip st in second ch from hook, sc in next ch, hdc in next ch, dc in next 2 chs, tr in next ch, dc in next ch, sc in next ch, slip st in same dc on Rose †; repeat from † to † for second leaf if desired.

Finish off.

SMALL ROSE (Make 3)

Ch 21.

Row 1: Dc in sixth ch from hook (**5 skipped chs count as first dc plus ch 2**), ★ skip next 2 chs, (dc, ch 2, dc) in next ch; repeat from ★ across: 6 ch-2 sps.

Row 2 (Right side)**:** Ch 3, turn; 4 dc in first ch-2 sp, skip next dc, slip st in sp **before** next dc, (5 dc in next ch-2 sp, skip next dc, slip st in sp **before** next dc) twice, 7 dc in next ch-2 sp, ★ skip next dc, slip st in sp **before** next dc, 7 dc in next ch-2 sp; repeat from ★ once **more**, slip st in last dc; finish off if desired, or work one or two leaves as follows:
† Ch 6, slip st in second ch from hook, sc in next ch, dc in next 2 chs, sc in next ch, slip st in same dc on Rose †; repeat from † to † for second leaf if desired.

Roll each Rose from beginning of Row 2, and tack on wrong side.

Using photo as a guide for placement, sew Roses to Border on one side of Tote.

General Instructions

ABBREVIATIONS

BPsc	Back Post single crochet(s)
BPtr tr	Back Post triple treble crochet(s)
CC	Contrasting Color
ch(s)	chain(s)
cm	centimeters
dc	double crochet(s)
dtr	double treble crochet(s)
dtr5tog	double treble crochet 5 together
FPsc	Front Post single crochet(s)
FPtr tr	Front Post triple treble crochet(s)
hdc	half double crochet(s)
mm	millimeters
Rnd(s)	Round(s)
sc	single crochet(s)
sc2tog	single crochet 2 together
sp(s)	space(s)
st(s)	stitch(es)
tr	treble crochet(s)
YO	yarn over

SYMBOLS & TERMS

★ — work instructions following ★ as many **more** times as indicated in addition to the first time.

† to † — work all instructions from first † to second † **as many** times as specified.

( ) or [ ] — work enclosed instructions **as many** times as specified by the number immediately following **or** work all enclosed instructions in the stitch or space indicated **or** contains explanatory remarks.

colon (:) — the number(s) given after a colon at the end of a row or round denote(s) the number of stitches or spaces you should have on that row or round.

CROCHET TERMINOLOGY		
UNITED STATES		INTERNATIONAL
slip stitch (slip st)	=	single crochet (sc)
single crochet (sc)	=	double crochet (dc)
half double crochet (hdc)	=	half treble crochet (htr)
double crochet (dc)	=	treble crochet (tr)
treble crochet (tr)	=	double treble crochet (dtr)
double treble crochet (dtr)	=	triple treble crochet (ttr)
triple treble crochet (tr tr)	=	quadruple treble crochet (qtr)
skip	=	miss

◼☐☐☐ BEGINNER	Projects for first-time crocheters using basic stitches. Minimal shaping.
◼◼☐☐ EASY	Projects using yarn with basic stitches, repetitive stitch patterns, simple color changes, and simple shaping and finishing.
◼◼◼☐ INTERMEDIATE	Projects using a variety of techniques, such as basic lace patterns or color patterns, mid-level shaping and finishing.
◼◼◼◼ EXPERIENCED	Projects with intricate stitch patterns, techniques and dimension, such as non-repeating patterns, multi-color techniques, fine threads, small hooks, detailed shaping and refined finishing.

CROCHET HOOKS																
U.S.	B-1	C-2	D-3	E-4	F-5	G-6	7	H-8	I-9	J-10	K-10½	L-11	M/N-13	N/P-15	P/Q	Q	S
Metric - mm	2.25	2.75	3.25	3.5	3.75	4	4.5	5	5.5	6	6.5	8	9	10	15	16	19

GAUGE

Exact gauge is essential for proper size. Before beginning your Tote, make the sample swatch given in the individual instructions in the yarn and hook specified. After completing the swatch, measure it, counting your stitches and rows/rounds carefully. If your swatch is larger or smaller than specified, **make another, changing hook size to get the correct gauge.** Keep trying until you find the size hook that will give you the specified gauge.

JOINING WITH SC

When instructed to join with a sc, begin with a slip knot on the hook. Insert hook in stitch or space indicated, YO and pull up a loop, YO and draw through both loops on hook.

JOINING WITH DC

When instructed to join with a dc, begin with a slip knot on the hook. YO, holding loop on hook, insert hook in stitch or space indicated, YO and pull up a loop (3 loops on hook), (YO and draw through 2 loops on hook) twice.

JOINING WITH FRONT POST SC

When instructed to join with a FPsc, begin with a slip knot on the hook. Insert hook from **front** to **back** around post of stitch indicated *(Fig. 4, page 46)*, YO and pull up a loop, YO and draw through both loops on hook.

BACK RIDGE

Work only in loops indicated by arrows *(Fig. 1)*.

Fig. 1

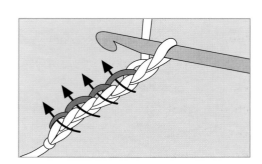

Yarn Weight Symbol & Names	LACE ⓪	SUPER FINE ①	FINE ②	LIGHT ③	MEDIUM ④	BULKY ⑤	SUPER BULKY ⑥	JUMBO ⑦
Type of Yarns in Category	Fingering, size 10 crochet thread	Sock, Fingering, Baby	Sport, Baby	DK, Light Worsted	Worsted, Afghan, Aran	Chunky, Craft, Rug	Super Bulky, Roving	Jumbo, Roving
Crochet Gauge* Ranges in Single Crochet to 4" (10 cm)	32-42 sts**	21-32 sts	16-20 sts	12-17 sts	11-14 sts	8-11 sts	6-9 sts	5 sts and fewer
Advised Hook Size Range	Steel*** 6 to 8, Regular hook B-1	B-1 to E-4	E-4 to 7	7 to I-9	I-9 to K-10½	K-10½ to M/N-13	M/N-13 to Q	Q and larger

*GUIDELINES ONLY: The chart above reflects the most commonly used gauges and hook sizes for specific yarn categories.

** Lace weight yarns are usually crocheted with larger hooks to create lacy openwork patterns. Accordingly, a gauge range is difficult to determine. Always follow the gauge stated in your pattern.

*** Steel crochet hooks are sized differently from regular hooks–the higher the number, the smaller the hook, which is the reverse of regular hook sizing.

FREE LOOPS OF A CHAIN

When instructed to work in free loops of a chain, work in loop(s) indicated by arrow *(Fig. 2a or 2b)*.

Fig. 2a

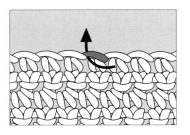

Fig. 2b

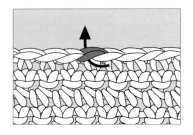

POST STITCH

Work around post of stitch indicated, inserting hook in direction of arrow *(Fig. 4)*.

Fig. 4

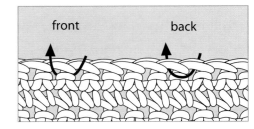

CROSS STITCH
(abbreviated Cross St)

Skip next st, dc in next st, working **around** dc just made, dc in skipped st *(Fig. 5)*.

Fig. 5

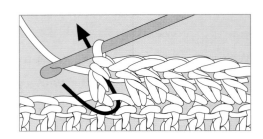

REVERSE SINGLE CROCHET *(abbreviated reverse sc)*

Working from **left** to **right**, ★ insert hook in st/row to right of hook *(Fig. 6a)*, YO and draw through, under and to left of loop on hook (2 loops on hook) *(Fig. 6b)*, YO and draw through both loops on hook *(Fig. 6c)* (**reverse sc made,** *Fig. 6d)*; repeat from ★ across.

Fig. 6a

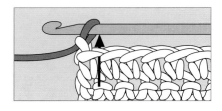

Fig. 6b

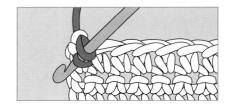

Fig. 6c

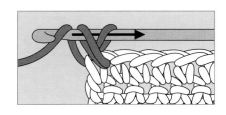

Fig. 6d

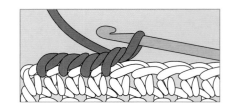

WORKING IN A SPACE BEFORE A STITCH

When instructed to work in a space **before** a stitch or in spaces **between** stitches, insert hook in space indicated by arrow *(Fig. 3)*.

Fig. 3

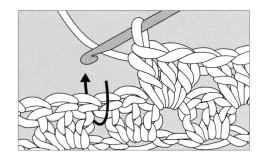

SURFACE SLIP STITCH

Surface slip stitch is worked on the right side of crocheted fabric and can be worked horizontally, vertically, diagonally or by following a chart. The slip stitches form a pattern on the **right** side of the piece, while the working yarn is held continuously on the **wrong** side. When working from a chart, each square represents one single crochet and the "ovals" indicate where a surface slip stitch will be worked.

With color indicated in instructions, make a slip knot (**Exception:** If you are working with a yarn that is still attached to the piece, begin working at the ★). With the **right** side of the piece facing, insert the hook from **right** side to **wrong** side in st indicated and place slip knot on hook at **wrong** side of the piece; pull the loop through to the right side. ★ Insert your hook from the **right** side to the **wrong** side (*Fig. 7a*), YO and pull loop through the piece **and** the loop on the hook; repeat from ★ for each additional st.

Fig. 7a

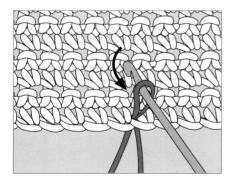

At the end of a row, cut yarn and pull the yarn to the **right** side through the last slip st made. To secure the last loop, thread a yarn needle with the end and insert it back through the fabric on the outside of the loop, pull yarn to the **wrong** side; secure end.

At the end of a round, cut yarn and pull the yarn to the **right** side through the last slip st made, insert the hook under the first slip st made, YO and pull end through (*Fig. 7b*). Insert hook from **wrong** side to **right** side through the last slip st made, YO and pull end through to the **wrong** side (*Fig. 7c*); secure end.

Fig. 7b

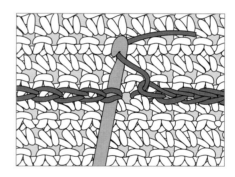

Fig. 7c

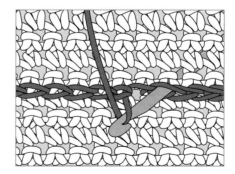

Yarn Information

The Totes in this book were made using Garnstudio Drops Paris 100% Cotton yarn, a medium weight yarn. Any brand of medium weight yarn may be used. It is best to refer to the yardage/meters when determining how many balls or skeins to purchase. Remember, to arrive at the finished size, it is the GAUGE/TENSION that is important, not the brand of yarn.

For your convenience, listed below are the specific colors used to create our photography models. If you plan on using Garnstudio Drops Paris 100% Cotton yarn, it will be necessary to order from the following U.S. distributor: www.nordicmart.com.

CAFFÈ LATTE TOTE
Off White - #17 Off White
Brown - #44 Brown

SUNNY DAYS TOTE
Grey - #24 Dark Grey
Lime - #39 Pistacho
Off White - #17 Off White
Rose - #38 Raspberry

TERRA COTTA TOTE
Beige - #26 Dark Beige
Brown - #44 Brown

TWILL WEAVE TOTE
Gold - #41 Mustard
Brown - #44 Brown

SUBLIME STRIPES SHOULDER BAG
Brown - #44 Brown
Orange - #45 Dusty Orange
Rose - #38 Raspberry
Lavender - #05 Light Purple
Lime - #39 Pistacho
Aqua - #10 Dark Turquoise

ARABESQUE CLUTCH
Black - #15 Black
Off White - #17 Off White

ALL-DAY SHOULDER BAG
Blue - #103 Dark Wash
Brown - #44 Brown

SHABBY ROSE TOTE
#17 Off White

Corrugated plastic (cake boards) can be found in the baking supply department of your local craft store.

We have made every effort to ensure that these instructions are accurate and complete. We cannot, however, be responsible for human error, typographical mistakes, or variations in individual work.

Production Team: Instructional/Technical Writer - Linda A. Daley; Editorial Writer - Susan Frantz Wiles; Senior Graphic Artist - Lora Puls; Graphic Artist - Victoria Temple; Photo Stylist - Lori Wenger; and Photographer - Jason Masters.